KU-726-465

ENGLISH SPELLING

Robyn Gee and Carol Watson

Designed and illustrated by
Kim Blundell

Contents

With thanks to Diccon Swan for his help and advice.

Why English spelling is difficult

English is used in many parts of the world as a first or second language, yet it is a very difficult language to learn.

There seems to be no logical pattern as to the way English words are spelt, and the way the words are pronounced often does not help either.

The reason why English is such an extraordinary language is that it is a mixture of many other languages.

Where do the words come from?

Long ago the British Isles were invaded by many different races, and each of these races contributed words to the language we now speak.

The Ancient Britons spoke a language called Celtic. Then Britain was invaded by the Romans who brought with them the Roman alphabet which we use today.

When Roman power declined, Britain was invaded by the Jutes, the Saxons and the Angles. Eventually their languages mingled to form Anglo/Saxon which is really the basis of the English language.

Next came the Viking invasions which introduced Scandinavian words; and finally there was the Norman Conquest which was very important as it introduced French into the language.

Over the centuries words from many other countries were gradually introduced into English as merchants travelled across the world, and scholars were influenced by the Renaissance. Latin and Greek were used by educated people, and for more than a century Latin was the only language recognized in English schools.

The British ruled in India for two hundred years and many Indian words have been absorbed into English from there.

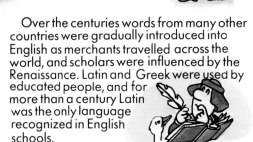

These words came from India.

thug

verandah   **bungalow**

More recently, our language has been influenced by the two World Wars and by American films and culture.

It is fun to discover where words came from. The study of word derivations is called *etymology.* Most good dictionaries provide a certain amount of information on etymology, but if you want a lot of detail you will need a special *etymological dictionary.*

Stories about words

In Roman times each Roman soldier was given an allowance to pay for the salt he needed. The Latin word for salt is sal. Nowadays there is an English word meaning "wages paid by the month or by the year". Do you know what it is?[1]

During the Middle Ages in England the pilgrims going to Canterbury used to ride at a gentle gallop known as the "Canterbury gallop". There is now a six-letter word to describe this gallop. Can you think what that is?[2]

There are lots of stories about words. See if you can discover some more.

Words from names

Some of the words we use now are connected with the names of people or places.

Sardines are so called because they are caught off the shores of Sardinia.

Wellington boots are named after the 1st Duke of Wellington who wore very high boots covering his knees.

The 4th Earl of Sandwich was an English nobleman who loved hunting. One day he hunted for twenty-four hours without stopping, and the only food he ate was meat placed between slices of bread. Food eaten like this has been called after him ever since.

[1] salary   [2] canter

How we spell

The first thing usually learnt at school is the alphabet. The English alphabet is made up of twenty-six letters. Five of these letters are called vowels – a e i o u. The other twenty-one letters are called consonants – b c d f g h j k l m n p q r s t v w x y z. The letter y can act as a consonant or a vowel depending on its position in a word.

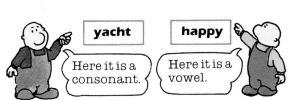

| yacht | happy |

Here it is a consonant.

Here it is a vowel.

Every word has a vowel letter in it. Try to remember this when you are writing.

Sounds

Each vowel letter has a short and long sound. (The long sound is the name of the letter.)

cat pen dig log tub

These are short vowel sounds.

mane these tide home tube

These are long vowel sounds.

The dictionary shows you which are short or long sounds by using special marks. *

Some words are easy to spell because each letter stands for a sound.

c-a-t spells cat.

This is easy.

Letters can, however, be combined in different ways to make many sounds.

ea oa ee ou ch sh th ck

Some letter combinations make the same sound.

oi oy   ea ee

This is when it becomes tricky. Many words or parts of words *sound* the same but are spelt differently.

pain pane | **buoy boy**

*See page 7

Sometimes the combination of letters may *look* the same but *sound* different.

enough | **though**

These are things which you have to look out for and try to remember.

Syllables

Words are made up of one or more syllables. These are one syllable words:

pen   hat   pig   fat

These words are more than one syllable:

better | **sister** | **wonderful**

When you speak, you stress different syllables in different words. Most dictionaries will show you which syllable in the word is to be stressed most.

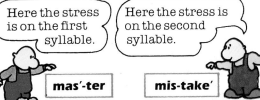

Here the stress is on the first syllable.

Here the stress is on the second syllable.

mas'-ter   **mis-take'**

ba-na-na

Some people misspell words because they miss out syllables. When you are not sure how to spell a long word try to sound every syllable as you write.

The pronunciation of words laid out in most dictionaries, and in this book, is the standard one (without any accent) and does not attempt to deal with regional accents in any way.

Rules

There are certain spelling rules to help you learn English spelling. Unfortunately, there are so many exceptions to the rules that you wonder whether it is worth learning them in the first place. However, it is better to have some guide than no guide at all. In this book, the rules are laid out as simply and as clearly as possible to provide the guidelines. The rules have pink boxes round them to make them easy to spot.

Using a dictionary

If you want to improve your spelling it is very important to have a good dictionary, and to try to look up words whenever you are in doubt about how they are spelt.

Besides telling you how to spell a word, a dictionary tells you a lot of other things. It tells you what a word means, how to use it, where it came from and how to say it. All this information has to be squashed into as small a space as possible. To do this the people who write dictionaries use abbreviations, signs and symbols, and different kinds of type which helps to make things clearer.

Different dictionaries use slightly different symbols and abbreviations, so look in the front of your own dictionary to find an explanation of the code.

Below is an entry from the *Concise Oxford Dictionary*. The labels around it tell you what everything stands for and should help you to decode your own dictionary.

What a dictionary tells you

1. *Main entry.* The word *reindeer* is the main entry word. It is in darker type than everything else, so that it stands out clearly.

2. *Pronunciation.* The letters in brackets after the word *reindeer* and the accent over it are there to help you say the word correctly. See pages 6 and 7 for more information.

3. The letter *n.* is an abbreviation for the word noun. One word can be several different parts of speech according to the work it does in a sentence, so sometimes there are other letters after the word as well. They are:

    a. = adjective
    adv. = adverb
    conj. = conjunction
    v. = verb etc.

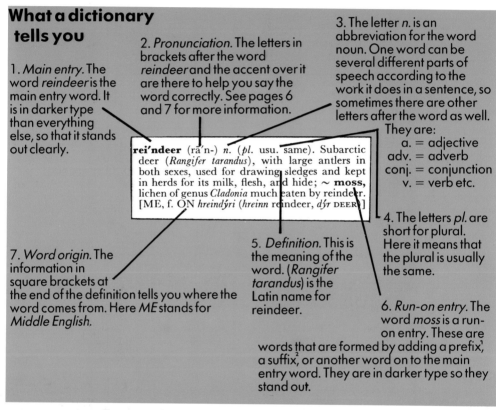

rei'ndeer (rā'n-) *n.* (*pl.* usu. same). Subarctic deer (*Rangifer tarandus*), with large antlers in both sexes, used for drawing sledges and kept in herds for its milk, flesh, and hide; ~ **moss,** lichen of genus *Cladonia* much eaten by reindeer. [ME, f. ON *hreindýri* (*hreinn* reindeer, *dýr* DEER)]

4. The letters *pl.* are short for plural. Here it means that the plural is usually the same.

7. *Word origin.* The information in square brackets at the end of the definition tells you where the word comes from. Here *ME* stands for *Middle English.*

5. *Definition.* This is the meaning of the word. (*Rangifer tarandus*) is the Latin name for reindeer.

6. *Run-on entry.* The word *moss* is a run-on entry. These are words that are formed by adding a prefix,[1] a suffix,[2] or another word on to the main entry word. They are in darker type so they stand out.

Using a dictionary to help you spell

How can you find out how to spell a word by using a dictionary? First of all you make a guess at the spelling and check to see if you are right. If you are wrong, make another guess and try again. Here are some useful hints to help you find the word you want.

1 All dictionaries have words listed in alphabetical order. The words are arranged firstly according to the letter they begin with. When two words begin with the *same* letter they are arranged alphabetically according to the second letter; and so on.

If a long word has the same first letters as a short word, but just goes on further, the short word always comes first.

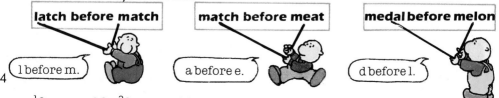

latch before match — l before m.

match before meat — a before e.

medal before melon — d before l.

[1]See page 18. [2]See page 20.

4

2

In English one sound can be spelt in many different ways. If your first guess is wrong and you are trying to think of another sensible guess, it might help you to turn to page 8. This suggests alternative ways in which the consonant sounds in your words might be spelt. If this does not help, look at pages 10 and 11 to see in what other ways the vowel sounds in your word may be spelt.

Here are some guesses you might make about how to spell "enough".

enuf	inough
enuff	enugh
enouph	enogh
enough	enouf

3

Some words have double letters where you don't expect them. Look out for these. You cannot always hear the difference between a double or single consonant sound, and so you can be caught out when you try to spell it. (See pages 8, 20 and 21 for guidelines to help you.)

This one is right.

unneccessary
unneccesary
unnecessary
uneccessary
unecesarry

4

Sometimes you may not be able to find the word you want because it contains a letter which is not pronounced, so you cannot hear it when you say the word. Letters which are not pronounced are called silent letters. They can be anywhere in a word. If you are having difficulty finding a word, turn to page 9 to help you decide whether it might contain a silent letter.

To look a word up it is very important to know what letter it starts with.

gnaw
honest
know
psalm
wrong

5

You may not find the exact word you are looking for as a main entry. Many words are formed by adding different endings, or "suffixes" (see page 20), to main entry words. If adding a suffix to a word alters the spelling in a way you would not expect, the spelling of the word plus its suffix may be listed in the run-on entries.

descending
descended
descends

Look up under "descend".

6

Some words consist of two other words joined together. They may be joined by a small mark called a hyphen, or simply written as one word. If you cannot find a word like this when you look it up, try looking it up in the run-on entries under the first part of the word. If this does not work, check the run-on entries under the second part of the word.

bookworm
song-thrush
ant-eater

Looking-up checklist

If you can't find a word in the dictionary, try:

1. Checking the consonant sounds on page 8 for for alternative spellings.

2. Checking the vowel sounds on pages 10 and 11 for alternative spellings.

3. Checking for silent letters on page 9.

Pronunciation and spelling

It is very important when learning to spell a word to say it aloud to yourself, so that your mind links the sound of the word and the feeling of saying it with the look of the word on paper and the feeling of writing it down. On this page and the one opposite are some suggestions on how you can make your pronunciation help your spelling.

1

If you come across a word you are not sure how to spell, it is often a good idea to break it up into *syllables* or sounds. A syllable is a part of a word pronounced as a single sound. It can form a complete word, or be part of a larger word and it usually consists of a vowel sound with or without consonants. When you split the word up into these separate sounds and say them slowly and clearly, you will often find that you feel more confident about spelling them right. This works well for words that are spelt more or less as they sound.

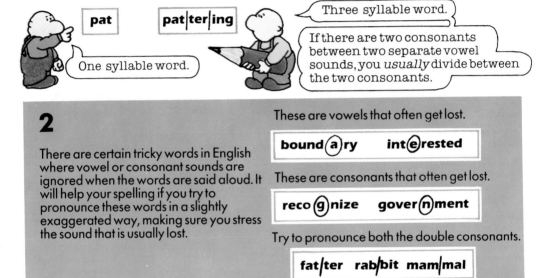

pat | **pat|ter|ing**

One syllable word.

Three syllable word.

If there are two consonants between two separate vowel sounds, you *usually* divide between the two consonants.

2

There are certain tricky words in English where vowel or consonant sounds are ignored when the words are said aloud. It will help your spelling if you try to pronounce these words in a slightly exaggerated way, making sure you stress the sound that is usually lost.

These are vowels that often get lost.

bound(a)ry   int(e)rested

These are consonants that often get lost.

reco(g)nize   gover(n)ment

Try to pronounce both the double consonants.

fat/ter rab/bit mam/mal

3

For words in which the pronunciation and the spelling seem to have little connection with each other, it is quite a good idea to have your own private way of pronouncing them to help you with the spelling. This can be very useful for words that have a silent letter in them.

Beware

draw✗ing   **saw✗ing**

Beware of certain words where an extra letter creeps into everyday pronunciation. The letter "r" is particularly inclined to worm its way into places where it should not be.

biskit
When you hear ...

bis koo it
Think, "Ah!" I know..

bis cu it
Real spelling.

nob
When you hear ...

ker nob
Think, "Ah!" I know ...

knob
Real spelling.

6

How a dictionary helps with pronunciation

1

If you are not sure how to pronounce a word correctly, a dictionary can be very helpful. A good dictionary will show how words are normally spoken, by using a system of signs and symbols. Pronunciation can, of course, vary from one region or country to another.

Radio and TV have helped to establish a standard or "received" pronunciation.

Dictionaries give what is called "received pronunciation". This is what most people would recognize as "good English".

2

Most dictionaries give a pronunciation guide for vowels, consonants and certain groups of letters, in the introduction. For words that present particular difficulties a dictionary often gives a respelling of the whole word, or just the difficult bit, in brackets after the word. The respelling is given in "phonetic" spelling based on a phonetic alphabet. A phonetic alphabet is a special kind of alphabet in which each letter, symbol or group of letters always represents the same sound, so that there is no confusion about what sound is written down. The phonetic system used by the dictionary should also be explained in the introduction.

conscientious (-shǐĕnshus)

Phonetic system:

sh = sh as in ship
ǐ = i as in bit
ĕ = e as in net
n = n as in net
u = u as in bonus
s = s as in sip

Most phonetic systems stay as close as possible to the normal alphabet.

3

Each of the five vowels in the alphabet can be pronounced in many different ways. Most dictionaries use a system of marks over vowels to help show the correct pronunciation. The key to these marks should appear in the explanation of the phonetic system in the introduction.

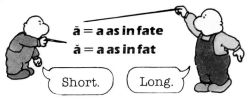

ā = a as in fate
ă = a as in fat

Short.   Long.

4

In long words, one or more of the syllables usually has more stress or emphasis on it than the others. Dictionaries normally show which is the most strongly sounded syllable by putting an accent, a comma or a stop after the stressed syllable. Some dictionaries divide their main entry words into syllables.

co'nsonant
a'lphabet
vow'el

Beware

Be careful with the spelling of these two words:

I *pronounce* words clearly.

But

My *pronunciation* is clear.

No "o" here.

What is the real spelling?

These words are written according to their phonetic spelling in the *Concise Oxford Dictionary*. Do you know how each of them is really spelt?

1. āk   6. prĕ'shus
2. bihāvyer 7. ka'rǐj
3. bǐ'znis   8. sǐ'zerz
4. for'ǐn   9. stŭ'mak
5. nŏ'lij   10. hăng'kerchǐf

7

Consonant sounds

Many sounds in English can be spelt in different ways. Below is a chart showing the consonant sounds that can be spelt in several ways and the different ways of spelling them. If you are having difficulty spelling a word or finding it in the dictionary, you may find it useful to look up the sound you want in this chart.

F The sound "f" as in *fall* can be spelt:

1. "f" as in *frog*
2. "ff" as in *giraffe*
3. "gh" as in *laugh*
4. "ph" as in *pheasant*

G The sound "g" as in *grab* can be spelt:

1. "g" as in *goat*
2. "gg" as in *egg*
3. "gh" as in *ghost*
4. "gu" as in *guitar*

J The sound "j" as in *jog* can be spelt:

1. "dg" as in *fudge*
2. "g" as in *giant*
3. "j" as in *joke*

K The sound "k" as in *kill* can be spelt:

1. "c" as in *cat*
2. "cc" as in *accordion*
3. "ch" as in *echo*
4. "ck" as in *duck*
5. "k" as in *king*
6. "qu" as in *bouquet*
7. "que" as in *cheque*

S The sound "s" as in *salute* can be spelt:

1. "ce" as in
2. "s" as in *snake*
3. "sc" as in *scent*
4. "ss" as in *hiss*

SH The sound "sh" as in *shoot* can be spelt:
1. "ch" as in *machine*
2. "ci" as in *special*
3. "s" as in *sugar*
4. "sh" as in *shampoo*
5. "si" as in *pension*
6. "ssi" as in *mission*
7. "ss" as in *pressure*
8. "ti" as in *nation*

Z The sound "z" as in *zoom* can be spelt:

1. "s" as in *daisy*
2. "z" as in *lazy*

Hard and soft "c"s and "g"s

The letters "c" and "g" can be either soft (*cinema*, *giant*) or hard (*card*, *gap*). The soft "g" sounds like a "j"; the soft "c" sounds like an "s". Both letters are only soft when they are followed by an "e", an "i" or a "y".

gem	**gin**	**gym**
garden	**gum**	**good**

celery	**cider**	**cycle**
cactus	**corn**	**cucumber**

Double letters

It is often difficult to hear any difference in sound between a single or double consonant. One useful guideline is to think about the sound of the vowel before it. *Double* consonants in the middle of a word *usually* only appear after a *short* vowel sound.*

These are all short vowel sounds.

matter
poppy
puppy

These are all long vowel sounds.

later
pony
pupil

*See pages 3 and 10.

Silent letters

English words are full of silent letters. These letters are not pronounced but must always be written.

You may wonder why these silent letters are there in the first place. The answer is that they used to be pronounced. In the Middle Ages all the consonants and most of the silent "s"s were still being sounded. Gradually, as pronunciation changed, some of the letters became silent.

Here are some examples of silent letters and words containing them.

Collecting words with silent letters

If you have a spelling notebook, it is a good idea to make a collection of words with silent letters. Use a different page for each separate silent letter and add words as you come across them.

Silent W
wr   wh
wren   whoever
wrinkle   wholewheat
wriggle   whom

B (after "m")
lamb   bomb
thumb   comb

(before "t")
debt   subtle

E An "e" on the end of a word is not usually pronounced. Many words have a silent "e" on the end.
The silent "e" usually makes the previous vowel long, if there is only one consonant between it and the previous vowel:

hat   hate

G (always before "n")
gnat   gnome   sign

GH
(at the end of a word)
weigh   though

(before "t")
bright   daughter

H (at the beginning of a word)
honest   hour   heir

(after "r")
rhubarb
rhyme
rhinoceros

(after "w" – in some accents, such as Scottish, you can hear an "h" when it comes after a "w")
whip
whisky

K (always before "n")
knot   knee   knife

L
half   calm   talk

N (after "m")
autumn   solemn
hymn   condemn

P (always before "s", "n" or "t". These words come from Greek)
pneumatic
pneumonia
psalm
psychology
pterodactyl

R
Sometimes "r" is not pronounced at the end of a word unless the next word begins with a vowel:
far   far enough

S
island   aisle

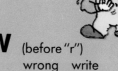

T (usually after "s")
whistle
castle
listen
rustle

(it is also hard to hear a "t" before "ch")
watch
fetch
itch

W (before "r")
wrong   write

(sometimes before "h")
who   whole

Vowel sounds

1 There are five vowels in the English alphabet. Each of these vowel letters, a e i o u, has two sounds:

a. A short sound:

| man hop pip tub pet |

b. A long sound:

| mane hope pipe tube Pete |

2 Dictionaries usually show which are short or long vowel sounds by putting different marks above the vowel letter to show you how to pronounce it.

hăd
băd
lĭp

This is the sign for a short vowel.

shīne
hāte
tūne

This is the sign for a long vowel.

3 You can make more vowel sounds by writing two or more vowels together, or by writing a vowel and a consonant together.

| boar   pier |

Two vowels.

| new half bird |

A vowel and a consonant.

Sounds chart

There are about 20 vowel sounds altogether in English and this chart shows you the most common ways of spelling them.

The sound "a" as in *hat* is nearly always spelt with an "a".

The sound "a" as in *skate* can be spelt:
1. "a" as in *gate*
2. "ai" as in *plain*
3. "ay" as in *crayon*
4. "ea" as in *steak*
5. "ei" as in *eight*
6. "ey" as in *grey*

The sound "a" as in *vase* can be spelt:
1. "a" as in *pass*
2. "al" as in *half*
3. "ar" as in *car*
4. "au" as in *laugh*

The sound "air" as in *fair* can be spelt:
1. "air" as in *chair*
2. "are" as in *share*
3. "ear" as in *bear*
4. "ere" as in *there*
5. "eir" as in *their*

The sound "aw" as in *yawn* can be spelt:
1. "a" as in *ball*
2. "al" as in *walk*
3. "augh" as in *caught*
4. "aw" as in *law*
5. "oar" as in *roar*
6. "or" as in *sword*
7. "ough" as in *ought*

The sound "e" as in *spell* can be spelt:
1. "e" as in *bed*
2. "ea" as in *bread*

The sound "ear" as in *disappear* can be spelt:
1. "ear" as in *dear*
2. "eer" as in *beer*
3. "ere" as in *here*
4. "ier" as in *pier*

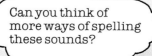

Can you think of more ways of spelling these sounds?

The sound "ee" as in *see* can be spelt:
1. "e" as in *demon*
2. "ea" as in *eat*
3. "ee" as in *keen*
4. "ei" as in *ceiling*
5. "ey" as in *key*
6. "i" as in *sardine*
7. "ie" as in *field*

the sound "er" as in *jerk* can be spelt:
1. "er" as in *earn*
2. "er" as in *service*
3. "ir" as in *bird*
4. "or" as in *word*
5. "our" as in *journey*
6. "ur" as in *nurse*

The sound "i" as in *sit* can be spelt:
1. "i" as in *pin*
2. "ui" as in *build*
3. "y" as in *pyramid*

The "i" before "e" rule

One of the vowel sounds that people most frequently get wrong is the "ee" sound. Here is a rule to help you..

"i" before "e" except after "c" when the sound is "ee".

These are "i" before "e" words.

achieve	field
believe	grief
brief	piece
chief	shield
thief	siege

ceiling
deceive
conceit
receive
perceive

These are "e" before "i" words.

The most common exceptions to this rule are: seize, weir, weird.

Y as a vowel

The letter "y" is sometimes used as a vowel depending on its position in a word. When it is placed at the beginning of a word it usually acts as a consonant. If it is at the end of a word, or if it has an "i" sound, it acts as a vowel.

Here it is a vowel.

yoyo   yacht

Wye valley

The sound "i" as in *drive* can be spelt:
1. "i" as in *dime*
2. "igh" as in *high*
3. "ie" as in *pie*
4. "ye" as in *goodbye*
5. "y" as in *cry*

the sound "o" as in *hop* can be spelt:
1. "a" as in *wasp*
2. "au" as in *sausage*
3. "o" as in *blot*
4. "ou" as in *cough*

The sound "o" as in *poke* can be spelt:
1. "o" as in *bone*
2. "oa" as in *soap*
3. "oe" as in *toe*
4. "ow" as in *blow*

The sound "ow" as in *frown* can be spelt:
1. "ou" as in *cloud*
2. "ow" as in *clown*

The sound "oy" as in *boy* can be spelt:
1. "oi" as in *coin*
2. "oy" as in *toy*

The sound "u" as in *duck* can be spelt:
1. "o" as in *come*
2. "ou" as in *young*
3. "u" as in *much*

The sound "u" as in *push* can be spelt:
1. "oo" as in *book*
2. "ou" as in *would*
3. "u" as in *bull*

The sound "u" as in *rule* can be spelt:
1. "ew" as in *screw*
2. "o" as in *do*
3. "oo" as in *shoot*
4. "ou" as in *soup*
5. "u" as in *flute*
6. "ui" as in *fruit*

The sound "u" ("you") as in *use* can be spelt:
1. "ew" as in *new*
2. "u" as in *duty*

The words above have a "y" sound in front of the "u".

The sound "ore" as in *more* can be spelt:
1. "oor" as in *poor*
2. "our" as in *tour*
3. "ur" as in *jury*
4. "ure" as in *sure*

Make a list of any more words that have this sound.

Words which sound alike HOMOPHONES

There are many words which sound alike but are spelt differently. Words that sound alike are called *homophones*. (The word homophone means "the same sound".) You will come across a great many *pairs* of homophones, but you will also find some groups of three or more words with the same sound but different meanings and spellings. Try to spot homophones and make a list of which spelling goes with which meaning.

> This is a prefix* which means "the same".

 read   reed   **boy   buoy**

Try these

Here are ten sets of the most common homophones. Can you fit them into the sentences correctly?

1. hear/here	1. "Come over . . . . . .," called Fred, but Alice was so busy she didn't . . . . .
2. new/knew	2. No-one . . . . . the people who had moved into the . . . . . house.
3. no/know	3. " . . . . . , I don't . . . . . the answer to your question.
4. past/passed	4. The girl . . . . . out as her favourite pop star went . . . . .
5. right/write	5. Most people . . . . . with their . . . . . hand.
6. weather/whether	6. Even the . . . . . man couldn't tell . . . . . it was going to be wet or fine.
7. which/witch	7. The silly . . . . . forgot . . . . . spell to use.
8. wood/would	8. He told us he . . . . . be moving to a house on the edge of a . . . . .
9. where/wear	9. She didn't know . . . . . they were going, or what she should . . . . .
10. to/too/two	10. . . . . . of the boys were . . . . . young . . . . . go . . . . . the football match.

Apostrophe muddle

Apostrophes are often used to make two words into one. When this happens the word formed can sometimes sound like another word. Make sure you do not confuse the words on the left below with their sound-alike words on the right.

> On the end of another word.

they're (they are)	— there
	their
it's (it is, it has)	— its
you're (you are	— your
who's (who is)	— whose
've (have)	— of

> These words are all possessive adjectives — they show that something belongs to something else.

12

*See pages 18 and 19.

Nouns and verbs which sound alike

Do you know the difference between these pairs of words?

practise	practice
advise	advice
license	licence

You can *hear* the difference between the verb "advise" and the noun "advice". Remember how to spell these words and it will help you with others like them.

The words on the left are verbs; the ones on the right are nouns. Look at the examples below to see how they are used.

**I practise my piano playing every day.
I need more practice at using the pedals.**

The verbs are spelt with an "s". The nouns are spelt with a "c".

**I advise you to be more careful.
I always give you good advice.**

**I am licensed to drive a car.
I have lost my driving licence.**

Meter or metre?

A "meter" is an instrument that measures something like gas, electricity, water or parking.

A speedometer measures speed.

A thermometer measures temperature.

A "metre" is a unit of length. The ending "metre" is used for all lengths based on the metre: kilometre, centimetre and millimetre.

The Americans use the word "meter" where the English use "metre". Don't let this confuse you.

Puns

A pun is a saying or sentence which makes use of homophones in a funny or clever way. Newspaper headlines, advertising slogans and some jokes and riddles are often puns.

Teacher: "**No fighting allowed in here!**"

Pupil: "**We weren't fighting aloud sir, we were fighting quietly.**"

"**Have you heard the story about the peacock? . . . It's a beautiful tale (tail).**"

Spot the mistakes

There are 13 mistakes in the sentences below. Can you find them all?

1. Cynthia had such a pane in her heal it maid her grown.
2. Fred was so greedy he ate a hole current cake without offering anyone else a peace.
3. Tom had such huge mussels he could lift too cars with his bear hands.
4. The drunkard spent the night in a prison sell and was find for using fowl language.

Plurals

A singular word is a word which refers to one thing or group of things; a plural word refers to more than one thing. When singular words become plural they change their spelling slightly to show the difference in their meaning. The way they change depends on what letter they end with in the singular.

The plural of most words is formed by adding "s" to the singular.

Words ending in hissing sounds

Words ending in "s" and other hissing sounds such as "sh", "tch", "x" and "z" take "es" to form the plural.

dress	dresses
dish	dishes
match	matches
box	boxes
waltz	waltzes

If you try to say these words in the plural by just adding an "s", you will see why you need to add an "e" before the "s".

Words ending in "ch" take "es" if the "ch" has a soft sound.

church
churches

Here you don't need an "e" to make the plural sound different from the singular.

If the "ch" has a hard sound, like a "k", you just add "s".

monarch
monarchs

If the hissing sound is followed by an "e", you just add an "s".

rose
roses

Test yourself

Can you change all these words into the plural using the above rules to help you?

1. address	7. lash	13. tax
2. garden	8. princess	14. table
3. case	9. pitch	15. arch
4. loss	10. dish	16. house
5. wish	11. ship	17. torch
6. march	12. crash	18. splash

Words ending in "y"

If there is a vowel before the "y", just add "s" to form the plural.

If there is a consonant before the "y" change the "y" to "i" and add "es".

Singular		**Plural**	**Singular**		**Plural**
vowel + y		+ s	consonant + y		+ ies
boy		boys	puppy		puppies

Any kind of name ending in "y" takes "s" in the plural, even if there is a consonant before the "y", so that the name will not be changed.

"Do you know Mr and Mrs Henry?"
"Yes, I know the Henrys."

Helpful hint! Pick on a word ending in "y", whose plural you already know, e.g. boy (boys). From this you can easily work out that it must be consonant + y that ends in "ies".

Add the right ending

Can you make these "y" words plural?

1. toy
2. misery
3. donkey
4. deputy
5. country
6. quay
7. memory
8. jelly
9. tray
10. robbery

Words ending in "o"

Most words ending in "o" make their plural by adding "s".

piano   pianos

But here are some words that end in "oes" in the plural. There is no rule to help you to tell which words end in "oes"; you just have to try to remember them.

There are also some words that can end in either "os" or "oes". You cannot go wrong with these. Use whichever ending you think looks best.

Try to remember these words.

buffaloes
cargoes
dominoes
echoes
heroes
mosquitoes
potatoes
tomatoes

Eskimos or Eskimoes
flamingos or flamingoes
halos or haloes
mementos or mementoes
mottos or mottoes
zeros or zeroes

15

Words ending in "f", "fe" and "ff"

Most words drop the "f", or "fe", and add "ves" in the plural.

leaf
leaves

If you say them aloud you can always hear which words end in "ves".

A few words just add "s" to form the plurals.

dwarfs	proofs
chiefs	roofs
griefs	beliefs

Take your pick.

Four words can be spelt either "fs" or "ves".

hoofs	hooves
turfs	turves
scarfs	scarves
wharfs	wharves

Which of these pairs are wrong?

Only some of these pairs of words have the correct plural. Can you pick out the *wrong* ones?

1. chief chiefs
2. roof roofs ✓
3. scarf scarves ✓
4. calf calfs *calves*
5. sheriff sheriffs ✓
6. knife knifes *knives*
7. leaf leafs *leaves*
8. wife wives ✓
9. proof proofs ✓
10. half halves ✓
11. tariff tariffs ✓
12. life lives ✓
13. shelf shelfs *shelves*
14. wolf wolves ✓
15. elf elfs *elves*
16. wharf wharves ✓
17. grief griefs ✓
18. cliff cliffs ✓
19. gulf gulves *gulfs*
20. mischief mischiefs
21. loaf loafs *loaves*
22. belief believes *beliefs*

Words with hyphens

Hyphenated nouns add an "s" to the main noun part.

son-in-law
sons-in-law

"Sons" is the most important part.

But where the nouns are formed from verbs, add an "s" on the end.

lay-by
lay-bys

"Lay" is part of a verb.

Words that stay the same

Sometimes the plural stays the same as the singular.

sheep	sheep
deer	deer
aircraft	aircraft

Complete change

Some words change their spelling completely in the plural.

mouse	mice
woman	women
tooth	teeth

Can you think of any more?

16

Latin words

Some words, which have kept their Latin form, take Latin plural endings.

Words ending in "us" change to "i" in the plural.	**terminus termini**
Words ending in "a" change to "ae" in the plural.	**formula formulae**
Words ending in "um" change to "a" in the plural.	**medium media**
Words ending in "is" change to "es" in the plural.	**axis axes**

Puzzle it out

What is the plural of:

1. antenna
2. cargo
3. axis
4. salmon
5. motto
6. brother-in-law
7. woman
8. buffalo
9. goose
10. piano
11. tomato
12. man-of-war

Use all the information to help you.

What is the singular of:

1. leaves
2. holidays
3. radishes
4. patches
5. echoes
6. kangaroos
7. courts-martial
8. opportunities
9. cities
10. hippopotami
11. abscesses
12. oases

Spot the mistakes

There are 13 mistakes in the story below. Can you spot them all?

One day the Kennedies went out for a walk, taking with them their dog and its two puppys. They wanted to get away from the noise of the cars, lorrys and busess; so they headed towards the open fields.

The leafs on the trees rustled in the breeze and the sun shone down on the rooves of the houses. As they drew nearer to the countryside, the dog chased butterflys and the puppys yapped at some donkies which were peering through the bushs.

At last the family reached the river and sat down to eat their picnic lunchs. Unfortunately, as they ate some tomatos they were attacked by a swarm of mosquitos.

17

Adding to the beginning of words

A prefix is a group of letters which can be added on to the front of other words to change their meaning. Prefixes have their own meanings (they usually come from Latin and Greek words), which become part of the meaning of the new word. If you know the meaning and spelling of some of the most common prefixes, it can help you to work out the meaning and spelling of a great many of the words we use.

"Pre" is a prefix. It means before.

A prefix is something you fix before another word.

Most dictionaries list prefixes as main entry words and give their meanings.

Here are some of the more common prefixes with their meanings:

bi focal

ad vance

appear

re

ab-	away, from		per-	through, thorough
ad-	to, into		poly-	many
ante-	before		post-	after
anti-	against		pro- ⎫	in favour of, forwards, in front
com-	with, together		pur- ⎭	onwards,
de-	down, below, off		re-	again, back
dia-	through, across		sub-	below
en- ⎫	in		super- ⎫	over, beyond
in- ⎭			sur- ⎭	
epi-	upon, above		syn-	with, together
ex-	out, away		tele-	far away
hyper-	above, greater			
hypo-	below, lesser		uni-	one
inter-	between		bi-	two
mal-	bad		tri-	three

Opposite meanings

A prefix is often added to give the opposite meaning to a word. All the prefixes on the right give the meaning of "not", "opposite of", "without". They are called *negative* prefixes.

dis-	non-
in-	un-
mis-	

Test 1   Can you add the right prefixes to the words below?

dis or de	*dis or mis*	*ante or anti*
part	take	natal
agreement	understanding	septic
lay	please	climax
obedient	satisfied	chamber
im or il	*un or in*	*pre or pro*
legal	discreet	ceed
moral	reliable	pare
logical	expensive	caution
possible	important	vide

Remember this rule

The rule about spelling words with prefixes is quite easy to remember:

> You do not change the spelling of a word when adding a prefix to it.

dis + solve = dissolve

Even when the last letter of the prefix is the same as the first letter of the word you are adding it to, don't miss out any letters.

mis + spell = misspell

You need both "s"s here.

All and well are exceptions

When you add "all" or "well" to the front of other words, they only have one "l".

all + together = altogether

well + come = welcome

All's well, if there's only one "l".

Prefixes in disguise

Do these words have prefixes?

arrange	collect	suffer
illegal	irregular	suppose

Many words in common use have prefixes that you might not recognize as prefixes. This is because some prefixes which end in a consonant change according to the word they are attached to — usually to make them easier to pronounce. The last letter of the prefix normally changes to become the same as the first letter of the base word:

ad- can become ac-, af-, ag-, al-, an-, ap-, ar-, as-, at-

com- can become col-, cor-, con-

in- can become il-, im-, ir-

sub- can become suc-, suf-, sug-, sup-, sur-, sus-

Test 2 What does the prefix in front of each of these words mean?

*ad*vance
*de*scend
*super*vise
*bi*lingual
*sub*merge
*mal*formation
*en*trance
*ex*it

Test 3 Can you make these words opposite in meaning by adding a negative prefix?

employment
fortune
respectful
pleasant
appear
responsible
alcoholic
patient

Adding to the end of words

A suffix is a letter or group of letters added to the end of a word to change the way you use it.

When you add a suffix to a word it shows the way in which the word is used and can change it from one part of speech to another.

She sat dream*ing* all day long. (verb)

This is the suffix *-ing*.

John is such a dream*er*. (noun)

This is the suffix *-er*.

If you know a little about suffixes it can help you to spell a word correctly.

Remember . . .

The spelling of a suffix never changes but the spelling of the word to which it is added sometimes does.

Below are some common suffixes and clues to how they are usually used.

-ary	-ly
-ery	-ous
-ory	-ic
-en	-like
-ish	-y
-less	-ful

These suffixes usually make adjectives.

-er	-ship	-ure	-ice
-or	-hood	-ance	-age
-ar	-ness	-ence	-ly
-re	-ism	-ment	

-ing	-ise
-ed	-ize
-ude	-yse
-ure	

These are often verb endings.

These usually form nouns.

Doubling trouble

When you add a suffix beginning with a vowel to a word which ends in one consonant, you sometimes have to *double* the consonant.

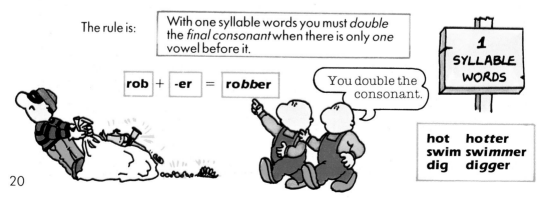

The rule is:

With one syllable words you must *double* the *final consonant* when there is only *one* vowel before it.

rob + **-er** = **ro*bb*er**

You double the consonant.

1 SYLLABLE WORDS

hot	ho*tt*er
swim	swi*mm*er
dig	di*gg*er

If a one syllable word has *two* vowels or ends in *two* consonants you just add the suffix.

No doubling here.

feel feeling
cool cooled
wreck wreckage

Doubling in long words

MORE THAN 1 SYLLABLE WORDS

Words with more than one syllable sometimes follow the rule for one syllable words depending on how the word is pronounced.

Look at these words.

gallop

begin

They both have two syllables, but they still have *one final consonant* with *one vowel* before it. If you add the suffix -ing to these words *gallop* remains the same – *galloping,* but *begin* doubles the n – *beginning.* The reason for this is that they sound different. When you say "gallop" you stress the first syllable, but when you say "begin" you stress the second syllable.

So the rule is:

> a. If the stress is on the first syllable there is *one consonant* before the suffix.
> b. If the stress is on the second syllable there are *two consonants* before the suffix.

Think which part of the word you stress most.

óffer offering
fásten fastened
propél propelling
forbíd forbidden

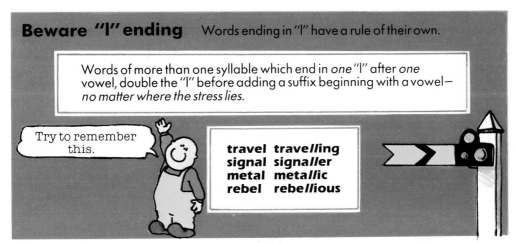

Beware "l" ending   Words ending in "l" have a rule of their own.

> Words of more than one syllable which end in *one* "l" after *one* vowel, double the "l" before adding a suffix beginning with a vowel— *no matter where the stress lies.*

Try to remember this.

travel travelling
signal signaller
metal metallic
rebel rebellious

21

Final "e" words

There are a lot of words which end in a silent "e". (Sometimes this is called a magic "e" or lazy "e".)

A silent "e" is never pronounced, but its presence at the end of a word can change the sound of the other vowel letter in that word from a short sound to a long sound.*

hat + e = hate	
cub + e = cube	
pin + e = pine	

> Adding a silent "e" can change one word into another.

Dropping the "e"

When you add a suffix to a silent "e" word you have to decide whether or not to drop the "e".

Try to remember this rule:

Drop the "e" when the suffix you are adding begins with a vowel.

hope	hoping
forgive	forgiving
love	loving

> Drop the "e" before a vowel.

Note. The letter "y" counts as a vowel when you add it as a suffix.

simple	simply
ease	easy

> This acts as a vowel here.

When do you keep the "e"?

Keep the final "e":

a. When a word ends in *ge* or *ce* before a suffix beginning with *able* or *ous*. You do this to keep the consonant sound soft.

notice	noti*c*eable
courage	coura*g*eous

b. To prevent confusion.

dye	dyeing
die	dying

c. When the endings *ye*, *oe* and *ee* come before the suffix.

eye	eyeing
hoe	hoeing
agree	agreeing

What about "ie"?

When a word ends in *ie,* change the "ie" to "y" before adding -*ing*.

die	dying
tie	tying
lie	lying

22

*See page 10.

Final "y" words

If you want to add a suffix to a word which ends in "y" you do have to follow certain rules.

Consonant here, change to "i".

If there is a *consonant* before the "y" change the "y" to an "i" and then add the suffix. If there is a *vowel* before the "y", just add the suffix.

marry	**mar*ried***
pity	**pi*tied***
enjoy	**enj*oyed***

Vowel here, leave the "y".

But if the suffix begins with "i", keep the "y" because you don't want two "i"s together.

study	**stud*iing***	✗
study	**stud*ying***	✓

Change the "y" to *ie* when you add an *s*.

beauty	**beaut*ies***
apology	**apolog*ies***

Beware

Words that are only *one* syllable *usually* keep the "y", except before *es* and *ed*.

fly	**flyer**
sky	**skywards**
dry	**dryness**

but* dri*es* dri*ed

Silent "e" quiz

What happens to the "e" when you join these words to the suffixes in brackets?

1. stone(y)
2. declare(ing)
3. excite(ment)
4. love(ing)
5. observe(ant)
6. manage(able)
7. advantage(ous)
8. lone(ly)
9. amaz(ing)
10. inquire(y)
11. hate(ful)
12. stare(ed)

Use the information on these pages to help you.

What about the "y"?

Can you add the suffix -ed to each of the words below remembering what should happen to the "y"?

1. copy
2. deny
3. dry
4. delay
5. ally
6. supply
7. obey
8. cry
9. prophesy
10. dismay
11. apply
12. stay

23

Double or single "l"?

It is often difficult to know when to write double or single "l", but there are some points to help you.

The *-ful* ending

a. Look at these sentences:

Emma felt *full of hope* when she started her new job.

Emma felt *hopeful* when she started her new job.

Notice that:

When you add *-full* to the end of a word you drop the last "l".

hand + full = handful
joy + full = joyful

There are two words which drop other letters as well.

awe + full = awful
skill + full = skilful

 Try to remember these.

b. When the suffix *-ly* is added to a word ending in *-ful* there *will be* a double "l".

tearful	**tearfully**
careful	**carefully**

Double or not?

When you want to add the suffix *-ing* or *-ed* to a word ending in "l" you should:

One vowel here.

Double the "l" if there is *one* vowel before it.

pedal	**pedalling**
travel	**travelled**

But don't double the "l" if there are two vowels before it.

fail	**failed**
feel	**feeling**

Try these

 Fill in the gaps.

Use the suffix *-ful* or *-fully* to complete the sentences?

1. Tom cheer . . . . . took the play . . . . . puppy for a walk.
2. Henrietta tear . . . . . gulped down a huge spoon . . . . . of the aw . . . . . medicine.
3. The bash . . . . . boy waited hope . . . . . for the beauti . . . . . girl to pass by.

Doubling test

Can you join these words and suffixes correctly?

1. patrol(ing)	6. feel(ing)
2. cool(ed)	7. expel(ed)
3. shovel(ing)	8. wheel(ed)
4. marvel(ed)	9. toil(ing)
5. appeal(ing)	10. fulfil(ing)

Tricky endings

It is easy to muddle up the endings of some words because they sound so similar. Some of them just have to be learnt but with others there are some useful tips to help you.

-able   -ible

These are two of the endings most often confused.

1. -able

> These two words both make sense as they are.

a. Words ending in *-able* can often be divided into separate words which make sense on their own.

> able + drink = drinkable
> able + adapt = adaptable

b, Words that have "i" before the ending usually take *-able*.

> rel**i**able   env**i**able   soc**i**able

c. You often use *-able* after a hard "c" or hard "g".

> edu**c**able
> navi**g**able
> ami**c**able

> These are hard letters.

d. When you add *-able* to a word that ends in "e", you usually drop the "e".

> love + able = lovable
> value + able = valuable

2.   -ible

> These words don't make sense on their own.

a. Words ending in *-ible cannot* be divided so that the words make sense on their own.

> sens + ible = sensible
> vis   + ible = visible

b. Most words with "s" or "ss" before the ending take *-ible*.

> respon**s**ible   permi**ss**ible   po**ss**ible

c. You often use *-ible* after a soft "c" or soft "g".

> le**g**ible
> eli**g**ible
> invin**c**ible

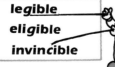

> These are soft letters.

Beware

There are some words that don't follow the above rules.

> Can you remember these? Some are quite difficult.

formidable	contemptible
inevitable	resistible
portable	collapsible
memorable	flexible
indomitable	

25

More tricky endings

-ery   -ary

very	bakery
brewery	nursery

Words ending in -ery are often obvious when spoken.

But there are some tricky -ery words.

People often miss the e sound out when they say these words.

cemet**ery**
monast**ery**
station**ery**

Watch out for these words.

Don't confuse   **stationery**   (paper, pens, etc.) and   **stationary**   (not moving).*

If in doubt about which ending to choose use -ary. It is more common.

January	dictionary
February	secretary

-er   -or   -ar   -re   -ure

These suffixes often sound similar and it is difficult to know which to choose. There are no rules to follow, but there are some helpful hints.

-or   This is usually used when the word means "someone who" or "that which".

A visitor is someone who visits.

-er   This occurs most at the end of everyday words.

mother
father
water
brewer
sinner

professor
survivor

-ance   -ence   -ent   -ant

a. You will usually find that the endings -ant and -ent are used for adjectives, while -ance and -ence are noun endings.

An import*ant* matter.

The import*ance* of the matter.

A differ*ent* opinion.

A differ*ence* of opinion.

These are adjectives.

These are nouns.

b. Certain consonants tend to be followed by a. The letters "t" and "v" often take -ance.

accept	acceptance
import	importance
relev-	relevance

Try to remember this rule. It may help you.

Every English verb which ends in r preceded by one vowel, and with a stress on the last syllable, forms a noun with -ence.

confér – conference
refér – reference
occúr – occurrence

26

*See page 12.

-ceed -sede -cede

a. Most words which end in this sound have the suffix *-cede*.

b. Only one word ends in *-sede*.

c. Very few words end in *-ceed*.

> **precede**
> **recede**
> **concede**

Only *one* word ends in *-sede*.

> **supersede**

> **succeed**   **proceed**

-ify -efy

Only four words end in *-efy*. All the rest end in *-ify*.

> **stup*efy***
> **rar*efy***
> **putr*efy***
> **liqu*efy***

Only 4.

-ise -ize -yse

Many of these endings come from Old French, Latin or Greek.
If in doubt use the suffix *-ise*. It is far more common than the other two.

> **surprise**
> **exercise**
> **disguise**

> **size**   **analyse**
> **prize**   **paralyse**

-le -el

Most words with this sound end in *-le*.

> **battle**
> **nibble**
> **trouble**
> **table**

75% end in *-le*.

but   **unravel**   **travel**
                    barrel

-ick -ic

Words of two or more syllables end in *-ic* not *-ick*.

-ick
(one syllable)
stick
thick
lick
trick
sick

-ic
(two or more syllables)
tonic
comic
static
artistic
fantastic

Fill in the ending
Can you add the right ending to the words below? Use your dictionary when in doubt.

-ary/-ery	-ify/-efy	-ent/-ant
1. confection . . .	1. ident . . .	1. observ . . .
2. annivers . . .	2. stup . . .	2. compet . . .
3. cemet . . .	3. fort . . .	3. defend . . .
4. comment . . .	4. spec . . .	4. superintend . . .
5. fin . . .	5. liqu . . .	5. brilli . . .

Other useful rules and tips

Here are some more words which are often mixed up because they sound or look similar.

accept	except	**I *accept* your kind invitation.** **Everyone went to the party *except* Doris.**
diary	dairy	**Tom always wrote everything down in his *diary*.** **The farmer's wife collected milk from the *dairy*.**
quiet	quite	**It was very *quiet* in the country cottage.** **Ben was *quite* good at football.**
legible	eligible	**James wrote the note in capital letters so that it was more *legible*.** **Jane was *eligible* for the job as she had all the right qualifications.**
affect	effect	**The shortage of water will *affect* everyone.** **The medicine did not have any *effect* for a week.**
lightning	lightening	**The thunder roared and the *lightning* flashed.** **She changed the picture she was painting by *lightening* the background.**
principal	principle	**The *principal* of the college had no *principles*.**

One word or two?

These are words which seem to confuse everybody:

Can you make up sentences to show how these words should be used.

Always two	Always one
thank you	today
on to	tomorrow
in front	together
in fact	tonight

Either one or two depending on the meaning

all ways	always
may be	maybe
no body	nobody
any one	anyone
all together	altogether
in to	into
some times	sometimes
every one	everyone

Did you know?

1. The letter "q" is always written as "qu". It never stands by itself.

   queen
   quarrel
   require
   inquest

2. No English word ends in the letter "j".

3. No English words ends in the letter "v" except the word spiv.

4. No English word ends in the letter "i" except for taxi (short for taxicab) and some words borrowed from Italian, e.g. macaroni, spaghetti and vermicelli.

Spelling games and puzzles

Crazy spelling

You can have fun taking words you already know how to spell and working out other logical ways of spelling them from the list of vowel sounds on pages 10 and 11, and consonant sounds on page 8.

A good example of this is:

What does this mean?

> **We had ghuiti on phrighdeigh.***

gh as in cough
ui as in build
ti as in nation

ph as in photo
igh as in high
eigh as in weigh

Try making up crazy spellings for the following words and then show them to your friends to see if they can guess the real spelling:

juice	flesh
cufflink	fluff
siphon	giraffe
coffeebeans	permission
golf	cashew

Computer games

There are now spelling games available to play on your own computer. Some of the most interesting ones are:

1. *Starspell* (BBC Machine, price £6.00)
2. *Witches Brew* (TRS 80 and BBC Machine, price £10.00)
3. *Spelling Builder* (TRS 80, price £12.50)

Dictionaries

Whatever game or puzzle you are playing, you will need to have a dictionary at hand to check your answers. Some useful dictionaries are:

1. *A Basic Dictionary* (Schofield & Sims Ltd)
2. *Oxford Elementary Learner's Dictionary of English* (O.U.P.)
3. *The Concise Oxford Dictionary* (O.U.P.)

*The answer is on page 31.

Palindromes

What do the words below have in common?

madam	minim
level	noon
rotator	radar
deed	civic

They are all *palindromes*. A palindrome is a word, phrase or sentence which reads the same backwards as it does forwards.

Here is a sentence palindrome. Some people think Napoleon could have said it.

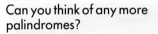

> **Able was I ere I saw Elba.**

Can you think of any more palindromes?

Word crosses and word squares

Look at the cross below. It is made up of two five-letter words which both have the same letter in the middle.

```
      S
      P
BUILT
      L
      T
```

How many word crosses can you make?

You can also make word squares using four five-letter words.

```
CLEAR
L    A
O    I
T    N
HANDS
```

The word at the top and the word on the left begin with the same letter (C), the last letter of the word on the left (H) gives you the first letter of the bottom word, and so on.

See how many more you can think up. Make up clues to the words and ask your friends if they can answer them.

Answers

What is the real spelling? (page 7)

1. ache
2. behaviour
3. business
4. foreign
5. knowledge
6. precious
7. carriage
8. scissors
9. stomach
10. handkerchief

Try these (page 12)

1. "Come over *here*," called Fred, but Alice was so busy she didn't *hear*.
2. No-one *knew* the people who had moved into the *new* house.
3. "*No*, I don't *know* the answer to your question.
4. The girl *passed* out as her favourite pop star went *past*.
5. Most people *write* with their *right* hand.
6. Even the *weather* man couldn't tell *whether* it was going to be wet or fine.
7. The silly *witch* forgot *which* spell to use.
8. He told us he *would* be moving to a house on the edge of a *wood*.
9. She didn't know *where* they were going, or what she should *wear*.
10. *Two* of the boys were *too* young *to* go *to* the football match.

Spot the mistakes (page 13)

1. Cynthia had such a *pain* in her *heel* it *made* her *groan*.
2. Fred was so greedy he ate a *whole currant* cake without offering anyone else a *piece*.
3. Tom had such huge *muscles* he could lift *two* cars with his *bare* hands.
4. The drunkard spent the night in a prison *cell* and was *fined* for using *foul* language.

Test yourself (page 14)

1. addresses	5. wishes	9. pitches	13. taxes	17. torches
2. gardens	6. marches	10. dishes	14. tables	18. splashes
3. cases	7. lashes	11. ships	15. arches	
4. losses	8. princesses	12. crashes	16. houses	

Add the right ending (page 15)

1. toys
2. miseries
3. donkeys
4. deputies
5. countries
6. quays
7. memories
8. jellies
9. trays
10. robberies

Which of these pairs are wrong? (page 16)

4. calf calves
6. knife knives
7. leaf leaves
13. shelf shelves
15. elf elves
19. gulf gulfs
21. loaf loaves
22. belief beliefs

Puzzle it out (page 17)
Plural endings:

1. antennae
2. cargoes
3. axes
4. salmon
5. mottos or mottoes
6. brothers-in-law
7. women
8. buffaloes
9. geese
10. pianos
11. tomatoes
12. men-of-war

Puzzle it out (page 17) Singular endings:

1. leaf
2. holiday
3. radish
4. patch
5. echo
6. kangaroo
7. court-martial
8. opportunity
9. city
10. hippopotamus
11. abscess
12. oasis

Spot the mistakes (page 17)

1. Kennedys
2. puppies
3. lorries
4. buses
5. leaves
6. roofs
7. butterflies
8. puppies
9. donkeys
10. bushes
11. lunches
12. tomatoes
13. mosquitoes

Test 1 (page 18) Add the right prefixes

depart	mistake	antenatal
disagreement	misunderstanding	antiseptic
delay	displease	anticlimax
disobedient	dissatisfied	antechamber
illegal	indiscreet	proceed
immoral	unreliable	prepare
illogical	inexpensive	precaution
impossible	unimportant	provide

Test 2 (page 19)

advance	—towards	submerge	—under
descend	—down	malformation	—bad
supervise	—above (over)	entrance	—in
bilingual	—two	exit	—out

Test 3 (page 19)

unemployment	disappear
misfortune	irresponsible
disrespectful	nonalcoholic
unpleasant	impatient

Silent "e" quiz (page 23)

1. stony
2. declaring
3. excitement
4. loving
5. observant
6. manageable
7. advantageous
8. lonely
9. amazing
10. inquiry
11. hateful
12. stared

What about the "y"? (page 23)

1. copied
2. denied
3. dried
4. delayed
5. allied
6. supplied
7. obeyed
8. cried
9. prophesied
10. dismayed
11. applied
12. stayed

Try these (page 24)

1. cheerfully, playful.
2. tearfully, spoonful, awful.
3. bashful, hopefully, beautiful.

Doubling test (page 24)

1. patrolling
2. cooled
3. shovelling
4. marvelled
5. appealing
6. feeling
7. expelled
8. wheeled
9. toiling
10. fulfilled

Fill in the ending (page 27)

1. confectionery
2. anniversary
3. cemetery
4. commentary
5. finery
6. identify
7. stupefy
8. fortify
9. specify
10. liquefy
11. observant
12. competent
13. defendant
14. superintendent
15. brilliant

Crazy spelling (page 29)

We had fish on Friday.

Index/glossary

abbreviation, 4 The shortened form of a word using some of the letters or just the initials: e.g. Feb. — February, C. A. Wilson.

adjective, 4, 20, 26 Describing word which gives a fuller meaning to a noun: e.g. *pretty* girl, *vicious* dog.

adverb, 4 Word which "modifies" or tells you more information about a verb. Usually answers the questions. How? When? Where? or Why? in connection with the verb.

apostrophe, 12 Punctuation mark which shows: (1) that one or more letters have been missed out: e.g. didn't; (2) possession.

conjunction, 4 Word used to connect clauses or sentences; or to connect words within a clause, e.g. and, but, or.

consonant, 3, 4, 6, 7, 8, 10, 15, 20, 21, 23, 26, 29 Any letter of the alphabet that is not a vowel (a e i o u). [When combined with a vowel forms a syllable.]

etymology, 2 Study of how words are formed and where they come from.

homophone, 12, 13 A word which sounds the same as another word but is spelt differently.

hyphen, 5, 16 Punctuation mark used to link two or more words together to make one word or expression.

negative prefix, 18 A prefix which, when added to the front of a word, gives it the opposite meaning: e.g. possible — impossible (see prefix).

noun 4, 13, 26 Word used as the name of a person, thing or place: e.g. dog, man.

palindrome, 29 Word, phrase or sentence which reads the same backwards as it does forwards: e.g. level.

phonetics, 7 System of spelling words by representing sounds by symbols.

prefix, 4, 18 Small addition to a word made by joining on one or more letters at the beginning: e.g. ex, pre, anti.

plural, 14, 15, 16, 17 A plural word refers to more than one thing: e.g. books, women, lilies.

pronunciation, 6, 7 The way you say words.

"received pronunciation", 7 The standard pronunciation "without any accent" used in this book and most dictionaries.

silent letters, 5, 6, 9 Letters which are present in a word, but are not sounded when the word is pronounced: e.g. knife.

singular, 14 The name referring to one thing or group of things: e.g. man, book, flock.

suffix, 4, 20, 21, 22, 23, 24 A letter or group of letters added to the end of a word to change the way you use it: e.g. coward*ly*

syllable, 3, 6, 7, 21, 23, 26 A combination of one or more vowels and consonants which can make one short word, or part of a longer word: e.g. cat, won-der-ful.

verb, 4, 13, 26 Word which shows some kind of action or being: e.g. run, jump, think, is, was, were.

vowel, 3, 5, 6, 7, 10, 15, 20, 21, 22, 23, 24, 26, 29 There are five vowels in the alphabet — a e i o u. All the rest are consonants.

The definition *reindeer* is reproduced from the *Concise Oxford Dictionary* (7th edition 1982) with kind permission of Oxford University Press.

First published in 1983 by Usborne Publishing Ltd, Usborne House, 83-85 Saffron Hill, London EC1N 8RT, England.

Printed in Portugal